No

film

in

the

camera

Hanne Bramness

No film in the camera

TRANSLATED BY
FRANCES PRESLEY
& HANNE BRAMNESS

Shearsman Books

First published in the United Kingdom in 2013 by
Shearsman Books
50 Westons Hill Drive
Emersons Green
BRISTOL
BS16 7DF

Shearsman Books Ltd Registered Office
30–31 St. James Place, Mangotsfield, Bristol BS16 9JB
(this address not for correspondence)

www.shearsman.com

ISBN 978-1-84861-268-6

Acknowledgements
The author and publisher wish to thank Cappelen Damm AS, Oslo, for
permission to publish this translation. These poems first appeared in the
collection *Uten film i kamaraet* (2010) published by Cappelen Damm.

This translation has been published with the financial support of
NORLA (Norwegian Literature Abroad).

Thanks to Andrea Moorhead for publishing
some of these translations in *Osiris* 74.

No film in the camera

1

One morning a bird sings in the top corner of a window on a branch high above the winter ground. On the sill a small conch lies in shiny sandwich paper and pipes in the draught. A catch has gnawed a wet groove, curled foil serves as a bowl for light. The paint is peeling off. Pools of dew swell with the coming of spring but it will soon freeze, because there is a sense of loss.

2

She is bending her head backwards so that half her forehead is outside the frame, her luminous breasts point straight up. She is singing or screaming. Dressed only in white winter skin, shoulders covered with hair that is electric. A folded umbrella and a lonely shoe by the door point in her direction, want to remind her that there is a world outside. The floor is partially erased by the light, it is still possible to set out and get across. It is still possible to pull back, run home and put an end to this experiment.

3

She has brought some props with her, a shabby shawl, a tortoise, a conch the size of a head. She has placed a worn sofa against a wall, hung up some transparent stockings, put a black feather and a thin knife on the sill outside the picture frame, stuffed a doll's suitcase too full, but still put it out. Things to aid her memory. Then she lies down with her back turned. Her face would have been wiped out anyway by the memory of pain.

4

Her slim figures are both sharp and unfocused.

Figures in motion, whether they are hiding in a bathtub, floating under the ceiling, lying undressed on the sofa, or sitting in a particularly awkward position in a fireplace. The motion reveals stagnation, the feeling of confinement. The pictures are of her and they are not of her, they are attempts to tear the body out of degradation, but its effect lingers on.

5

The figures are birds stretched out across the entire picture surface, even when they are standing in a corner. The rooms they move around in are hysterically cold, as if at any moment it could start snowing. When the steam from a bathtub draws such precise patterns in the air it reveals how cold it must be.

6

Although he has been lying in the yellow bathtub for several hours it doesn't matter because the water is still just warm, steam rising from it. Like a firm grip around the body, a body-glove, not too tight, but comforting. The water reaches up to the neck, liquid amber the same colour as the tub. Only the heated head with thin hair is visible in the picture.

7

The women in Rue Asselin are mostly out on the street, fully dressed. They have frocks, but the patterned fabric is hardly distinguishable from the flecked walls, the white stockings look like holes in the house façade. Pearl necklaces seem insistent, indecent like Christmas decorations in mid or late summer. The light reveals that the sun is going down. The sweat on their brows has dried out as if the photographer's presence has a cooling effect, their mouths are not smiling. Looking directly into the camera they are still turning away.

8

The smiling women on the tile floor in Alicante are twisting their naked sun bleached thighs, they keep wriggling one foot with a pointed shoe, without knickers or else ones that are too tight, stockings which gnaw at the hollow of their knees, bras that cut into their shoulders and give them two sets of breasts each, back and front. They are not only defiant and self-absorbed, but have already left.

9

The beach of Orissa, where Gandhi finally won the battle over salt, is perhaps the setting for this picture of newly dyed saris. They lie stretched out in an uneven check pattern. The fabrics seem heavier, much more durable than the women guarding them, as if it's the women who might rise and fly off to another beach in a gust of wind. Or perhaps they never quite landed? The same can be said of the boys in the white sunlight in Arsila. The shadows of the anchors in the sand, frayed ropes, dried fish offal, even their own shadows are not as elusive as they are.

10

In Rome the hairdresser is caught at the moment he rubs his almost hairless skull in the window of his salon. Suddenly part of his display, but as a health warning! He looks around, on his left the bleached curls of an open mouthed doll. But there is no tension in the picture, the focus is on the afternoon light, a matter of fact, mild light caught at the right moment.

11

If you wait for something to pass you do not wait in vain. For in the meantime there is a kind of peace, or so it would seem. Some rely on it so much they keep their secrets until they die. The surface becomes an idol for their sacrifice, love must be sacrificed for a picture of love. Photographers do not spend their whole lives taking photos in order to recall surfaces, but what has happened just before or long before, and what will happen immediately afterwards.

12

Most of the girls have plaits, some long, some short, like tiny plucked feathers. Some have one plait, some two, but it's best to have two joined into one, with a pastel bow that rubs against the gymslip. Whoever makes that sound becomes light-footed, straight-backed as a pine marten on two legs. It will soon be Christmas, the gym is reflected in ever darker windows. The girls with plaits wet from the snow are allowed to stand nearest to infinity and warm their thighs on the radiator. All pictures are equally precise.

13

There is such clarity in the photos that when the light falls obliquely you can see what a child observes reflected in his eye. That is when it becomes intimate.

14

In the Christmas photos light and stars catch the eye, a green reflection in black and white. Shaking their heads very fast the hair becomes a halo. When they danced around the Christmas tree she clasped the child's hand just hard enough that his face would not crumple and dissolve into tears. It doesn't matter that the child looks surprised, but why wasn't he beaming?

15

The two girls are photographed from behind, on their knees on the same old chair peering out of the window. The street and the rows of houses are already dark, but the sky is lit up and vast. Taken long ago, but the children are still leaning their heads together, neatly plaited, not a hair out of place. Their shoulders speak of their expectations. The presence of the photographer is not really a threat, but a substitute for one. It must be the weekend, at last, a break from eternity.

16

Light rains against the window on the first floor, drives through in waves and spills down the staircase. It drips from the banister onto the steps, gathering in swollen pools. A white winter light runs over, cascades and forces the children on the bottom step onto the floor where they lie and splash around, the back of their heads almost wiped out, their wrists and their ankles transparent, their faces aged. For they will always resemble their winter masks.

17

Some pick at their scabs, others lick them. Is the effect the same? Her mother sits heavy and deaf on the organ stool, she has married beneath herself. This is written on her face in all the pictures. What kind of small fry does the child then become? Her father is out fishing for carp to earn a living. Is this food for humans? He pulls and pulls. A carp can weigh over a hundred kilos. It can weigh three hundred. But in captivity, not out on the lakes. It is before Christmas.

18

The lake is covered with ice, a layer too thick for the boat. The fish swim so close that their dorsal fins rub against the transparent ceiling. This is how the fish become their own image.

19

She is an elegant, sad fish with a gaze that burns a hole in the picture, a reverse eyeful. The glass on the table is also eye-catching, upright on its own shadow looking as if it's about to take off. In the young woman's photographs no one smiles, not even with their eyes. There are many who will not dissimulate, they sacrifice their smile.

20

She is surprised in the shower by her mother, who discovers the blood blisters on her skin which, even in a black and white photograph, look blue, marks from an encounter with love. She blushes and smiles with her whole body, as much as she possibly can. But trying so hard does not inspire confidence.

21

The light in the picture is merciful. It brings out the dark shadows under her eyes. It lifts the oily fringe, strokes her brow, creeps behind some stray curls, screens them. The light grips her narrow hand with the dark cigarette, or is it a pen she is holding? Around her head light forms a watery halo where the foliage and wall behind her flow. It inflates one of her cheeks to a balloon, brings her the forgiveness she cannot give herself.

22

There is a boat on the window sill, not much bigger than a grasshopper, but the details are so finely crafted that if you go close up it looks huge *like a ship on its way to where the world ends*. As long as you remove the bar of soap lying next to it. But a short distance transforms it into a splinter.

23

When the water receded the sun got extra strength from the lake's mirror and the whole house creaked and quickly dried. Then it was aired and cleaned and in the end the living room seemed untouched. In the picture it's not possible to see how the books and papers whirled round with the frail furniture and a chopping-block that came in with the flood—pushing against the stove doing no damage—as impossible to read as the papers and books sailing past two feet under, but the high water mark just below the window reveals everything.

24

In the picture there is no smell. That goes without saying. Are we forced to state the obvious? When I look at the picture of the room on the island with a green shadow on the wall after the flood—the water had probably been there for a while—the smell hits me, reinforced by all that is lost, the house that is gone, and she has gone with it.

25

Hear the first frog of spring! Hear the musk rats gnaw on invisible logs in the water, it's a sign. When ice floats roar because they run with the current, the swans will soon arrive and settle. When the sun anchors by the pier so that the boards twist and crackle, when the first heron takes off and its cry disappears in the depths, when the surface receives all the sounds again and sends out answers, then a picture of the lake comes into existence.

26

One spring day by the Seine the wind starts blowing, so the makeshift tent they have gathered under, a round blanket stretched over some sticks, suddenly becomes a sail. He must fasten his grip, not only around the useless tent, but also around the women in dresses, and stretch out his arms to stop them rising up from the long grass on the bank and being lifted out over the water where summer gleams and beckons. He gets on his knees with his back turned. The wind fills his shirt, but it's easy to see that all his muscles tense, that he swears and rages not to be left alone.

27

The geese on the track of their lost shadows in the early summer at Beauce. In Holland, the pigs have clambered up and are sniffing with their snouts in the air for a warmer current. Lovers behind a crag in the Stockholm skerries, haloed by the rose light of spring. And in Paris by the bank of the Seine those pale from winter come walking over the ramparts to lap up the sun reflected in the river. An old couple in Ivry-sur-Seine settled by the water's edge, see the evening clear its way with golden wings—again. In Auila degli Abruzzi straggling blades of grass between worn flagstones. The photographer is hunting Europe's spring, along boulevard and pig sty, he wants to catch the light that deprives things of their value—meaning their place in a hierarchy.

28

The slim bottle-necks catch the residue of daylight in their funnels, the light caresses them. The corks are tight, but the content evaporates until suddenly it is full again as if someone had reversed the film. And even though the bottles cannot cast a shadow in this evening light, they do. Placed in the farthest corner of an overloaded trolley, they dominate and shatter domestic calm.

29

In the exact moment when she gets into the car, lifts her leg with the shiny boot and her skirt swings out like a foresail, just as she stretches her arm out for the wheel, takes a glance over her shoulder with her eyes closed, he is there and takes the picture. The church clock tower is reflected in the bonnet, but he cannot stop her or time itself, not even with film in the camera.

30

She goes out on a windless morning just before Christmas. Grey dawn light still lingers over the coast. She breathes deep and white. The path leading down to the beach stitches through frost-frail, almost invisible heather. Around a bend she runs into Jesus dressed in a cloak red as fever. Not the right colour for advent, and not what you expect. He leaves her again before the sun rises, but finds the time to forgive her. This is the season of winged demons.

31

She is naked. She wants to go out and down to the river to twist herself around the roots of a tree hanging over the water, she wants to get in the water and hear the silence. She is ready, but it is impossible. It has started to snow, an autumn has passed and another Christmas is over. If she flings a coat around her, nothing else, if she runs with her arms open, shaking her head to wake up, she still has no chance.

32

Naked but not with milk white skin or hair that tickles the waist. No thick plait to wave! Or to cover her breasts if necessary. Not the birthday suit of Eve or the Virgin Mary. She does not lie down and curl around an enamel bowl full of shiny eels, she does not hold a mask to conceal her cunt. She does not smile at the camera with a gaze that sees and does not see. Many of the female photographer's figures are young and introspective, but this woman is lying on the beach fully dressed, her pale frock soiled by the wet sand, her eyes closed and some grey lilies by her side. She is fifty years old.

33

In Europe, but beyond Europe, lies the Queyraz Valley. Here the snow is so deep that if someone falls through they will never reach the ground. But on the south facing slope and on patches of field by the river, the sun has blown into the water and softened the bank, exposing the grey earth and struggling blades of corn. And the red spots in black and white are thousand year old traces of Attila's men, their cries hang in red air along the sides of the valley. If there is no sky in this picture it is still an image of the heavens.

34

Thrusting buds in silver or wood. A root formed like a snow crystal suspended on a darkening sky. Swaying poppies and creeping ears of corn, in metal. Loosestrife with stiff, swollen joints. An artful leaf on a half-peeled branch about to unfurl—like a small girl naked to the waist and showering in the sun. In these pictures the subjects are doubly dead, objective lifeless forms that imitate life.

35

She was sitting down, forgetting herself, letting time and place slip in the splashing swarm of light and dark voices, white bodies, sun hats and dancing shadows on an English river bank, as if she belonged in a dream. Suddenly she gets up holding on to the pram which tilts over. It's empty! He takes her picture, just like the animal he captured, a hare crouching on the road frozen in the gentle headlights of a car that stopped, at the last moment.

36

The moon is a fugitive across wet rooftops, the streets are bridges that end in the sky, if you follow them until sunrise. He is out wandering with his camera very early or very late, when subjects are at their most exposed. He steals past some lovers in the narrow lane to the harbour and takes a snapshot. But even though he only uses the light from the streetlamp they are undressed. In the pub by the river a couple with restless hands and twisted lips are caught too, but saved by the tenderness of perspective.

37

In Sarajevo two small girls make their way, each with an oversized paper bag, in the chalk light that only whitewashed walls and sharp shadows can project. It is spring. They walk with such careful steps that they must be carrying eggs or rabbits. They are going left past the frame of the picture on a surge of warm sun that comes flooding back from the future. With their free arms wrapped around each other's shoulders they lean against each other so that they will not be swept off their feet by all that is to come.

38

She was never called mother, but Maar, and allowed to share his life for nine years. A portrait by Picasso, so significant in its style, is from a photo of her shadow on a whitewashed wall. She stands next to it, slim and shy, and her skin shines as if she has just washed in tears. That's why she is so difficult to grasp and hold fast. But her shadow is steady and mothering.

39

These roses seem pure and unscented with petals whiter than newly baptized sheets, resting cheek to cheek in a posy. If they are liberated from their stems the heads can survive for a while on their own, but before they succeed completely they will start to fall.

40

He is rough, made of wood, but his mouth and fingertips are glass, I can see that. They are smooth. Inside him volumes of water solidify, the water mirror is visible in the picture I develop with the aid of a small white flame. His profile is turned up like a foot about to dance, the shadow of his tongue behind the lip catches my eye. When my eyes take him in I am struck by many things, such as the light spreading across the back of his hand. I follow blindly.

41

Sunlight floods in. Someone has left open the red door to the desert, turned up the shutters of the light blue blinds, in a yellowing black and white. The dead tree in the garden draws spectral shadows in the room, at noon, they are pale shivering in the heat. The picture warns of a storm that will only take place in the one who looks.

42

On the first day of spring we see a pale brown boy turn the corner and run straight into the sunlight, weighed down by a litre bottle under each arm, luckily, because otherwise he is so thin he would take off. On the second day thirteen cloaked schoolchildren are standing high above the city waiting for the wind to take hold and blow them away in formation. But the photographer prevents this at the last moment. On the third day of spring, many years later, two pairs of shoes rest on the river bank while their owners find each other, sun warm hair against ice cold cheek, or vice versa. Smiles ripple their lips while the wind chases small waves on the surface of the water.

43

Wilting tulips in a warm hand, a tear in a ballet skirt, a cut in the red star, patent-leather shoes filled with chalk. He is searching for details that shine. In Leningrad in May an angry schoolgirl peers out from behind soldiers on military parade, her gaze wandering. On the circus poster from Texas a woman smiles, her pupils burnt out with a cigarette. Back in Paris where the spring sun blesses those it meets, the short open-mouthed bride on a swing has a missing tooth.

44

On bicycles through sun baked streets, down crumbling flights of steps, across market squares and bridges, rubbish strewn, derelict, they follow the route they will keep following until time runs out. They are cycling as if in a race, speeding up. Or they position themselves on stairs and roofs, with kites. They must have glass on the strings sharp enough to cut a rival's and give them victory in the kite wars. The sun beats on the roof as if it was a gong, but nobody wins.

45

On L'Isle-sur-la-Sorgue light drips from the trees. In the avenue that runs from one side of the island to the other, no one can be seen. But over an abyss of glassy ice a duck turns closer into the wind, which today is so feeble that the ancient maples barely flutter their new formed leaves. If a human being had entered the picture time would have accelerated.

46

The photo from the jetty will always be coloured by dark murmuring. Those who have met by appointment so early this morning stand unnaturally close together for strangers. Not enough light, but somebody still brought their camera to document these people for posterity before they boarded ship. How did they proceed up the gangway? Which of them grabbed hold of the railing? The crowd drifts apart, begins the journey. Hats cannot protect against the cold. The finery—silk stockings, rings, glossy suitcases—shines faintly. Under cover of remaining night the ship glides out, more quietly than in the picture.

47

In the southern sky the sun shines like a faint flare above obliterated roofs, in the foreground a black cross is enthroned with roses half drowned by snow. It is war time and some say that it must always be winter. But when frozen barbed wire shelters lovers and their kisses steam in the cold, something is not right. Along the ramparts wild cherry and chestnut are blossoming. The couple are lightly dressed, even well dressed, in a tight embrace on a chair somebody has set out. Under the barrier the gravel is freshly raked.

48

His shoulder is level with the ditch, gorse grows round him and crowns his invisible brow. His chest and the upper part of his stomach are out of focus. From where he lies his naked foot with the white nail fills half the sky like a moon made of glass. This is how he photographs himself as a soldier.

49

The children carry on with their war games, do not go to the beach on a sunny day, perfect for swimming, but instead pick up cartridge cases, percussion caps, red stumps of wiring, bits of concrete, and manoeuvre, in their Sunday best, a melted car without wheels on the edge of the city beyond civilisation. They sit there on the roof and stare at the horizon. Thirsty for images.

50

With school bags dancing on their backs, arms stretched out, heads turned around, t-shirts flapping and bright jackets. On a dusty road through arid heath land, in a landscape with no trees for shelter, past low fences and stone walls—with their hearts banging in their ears, a chirruping in their throats and feet like concrete in their sneakers, they run to catch up with the future. But they are still standing in the same spot with a view of their home on the horizon, conjured up by mist or floating above the ocean.

51

The way he holds the loaf makes it look as if he is stroking a cat, one they have threatened to take away because he is too young and hungry. And the way he stands on his head in the sand with a defiant stare, treading air with his naked feet, it becomes hard to decide whether he is a longed for child or the enemy.

52

Stiffly ornamental in identical shop-bought dresses, with puffed sleeves and velvet bows, under fading mulberry blossoms, knees pressed together to look slim, their bodies don't fit. They are staggering under the weight of the occasion. They are standing next to their grandmother who is just visiting and therefore fits in very well. She, who was like a daughter to her first husband, a sister to the second, a mother to the third and so on. Like the fruit on the trees the girls' hearts will soon form.

53

There is a rush of summer through the back garden, but it could be the high-voltage cable which does not appear in the photo. The foliage is dark grey. The girls are squinting at the camera. They have swapped their dresses for shorts which are too tight, but they look more at ease and childlike, arms around each other's sunburnt, thinly clad shoulders, carefully happy, almost. A cat presents its backside, tail sticking up. If they should send a photo into space as an example of our civilisation, it would hardly be this one.

54

When princess Mira lived on earth, wandering from town to town, barefoot, all her possessions in a bundle, no one caught her with a lens. No one lured a portrait from salt paper and sealed it with silver for posterity. But from the words she sang of fear in cloudbursts, of the tongue's lightning, of a girl who is driven too far or who seeks refuge in the depths where all secrets are known, the outline of a thin, ecstatic shadow emerges.

55

The girls lean against a house wall and the expression on their faces, their worn smiles, pale cheeks and fringes, match the late summer afternoon, as well as the flowery cotton dresses and sun-coloured legs that wade in shadow. They probably feel the heat from the wooden slats through the washed-out material, and so they are unbuttoned all the way down to the navel airing their breasts, pearl brown and white as flies' wings.

56

There is a portrait of a girl from Christmas in the jungle, pale as a small angel. In the background you can dimly see a bed or bunk, a spindly table, two stuffed birds, a jersey dress on a hanger, a lonely shoe on its way across the floor. The Christmas rain will drum against the corrugated iron roof, as drops glitter and run down her forehead and cheeks. It resembles a post-mortem photo in which the deceased was immortalized with their eyes open or pupils painted on the lids. But she survived childhood.

57

Through a jagged hole in a wall, which turns inward onto rooms that once existed, a long time ago, or not so long ago, perhaps a great crowd of children in white will appear in the ruins—some floating, some on crutches— but perhaps not.

58

She has landed here in the open doorway, the child
housewife from Bethnal Green, sliding in on soapsuds,
falling forward and kneeling down, balancing a heavy
dripping rag. With a swollen harelip and only two
stiff fingers on her right hand, she follows the rings of
bright suds on the step until they fade. Behind her floats
wallpaper with clouds.

59

The large breasts keep the slim body adrift. The water is so clear that on shore she would have seemed less exposed. The foot is a naked wing with which she keeps balance. The lake reflects the sky and she flies across it, as if the picture was taken upside down. And the forest is mirrored in the water so that she is always tangled in the branches.

60

It's night; the needles drip blots of blue. The green's out. As the moon becomes visible between clouds the green returns, but with a blue tint, reflected, reinforced by mute windows. Soft needles scrape against the glass. Close up you can't see what colour they are, but you can tell.

61

Seen from above it's as if she has been stitched into the floor, one long stitch around her waist and one round her upper arm. Captured at last, bent around a crumpled piece of cloth. Yes, finally held down, she rests with her head on the dark ground like a rain lashed peony. Drops are running along the arched spine to her neck, under the skin.

62

The shadow is either burnt into the floor or floats like a finely shaped flake of soot over the pale boards. It lies stretched out while its owner gets up and sits naked on a bench, hands between her knees, ready to slip away and set the shadow free.

63

They are naked jail-birds with thin fingers, pointed mouths. In the morning strip wash they are bobbing about by the edge of the enamel basins, moistening their faces and hair, borrowed plumage, and waving their tails a bit to shake off the water. Light caresses them, runs over their shoulders and white stomachs, down shiny thighs and arms full of deep scars.

64

The hairline meets the mountain ridge, the forehead is a precipice above a low, dark brow. A moustache covers the upper lip, but the lower lip is narrow and naked like a flayed root, his chin has a horizontal cleft. He is an angel with a third eye just below the skin. He is about to emerge from the landscape or to disappear, he oscillates, that's his nature. When night falls, the eye lights up like a white cone in the pine forest.

65

In the winter forest young trees pass down the mountain in formation, mumbling a dead language. Soon they have passed by, there are just some holes from thin roots in the frozen ground and patches of darkness in the light where they trod. Narrow rays slid over the trunks, tried to hold them back, but were defeated. The falling snow thickens. Soon all proof will be removed. Under its canopy the forest disintegrates, but is still the same.

66

She leans her head against the wall, presses her ear to it, strokes and taps it, to make sure that inside the wall time stands still. If she keeps still she will see a blurry speck expanding on the surface where a swan with a narrow beak and shiny black feathers sails towards her. It will not stop until it is so close that it touches the palm of her hand, a sign, a mark of affinity.

67

She hangs like a bat in the doorway and represents an angel, with clothes pegs in her skin. Her hair partly erased, glued to the doorframe in clumps. Her legs are like the tail of a wriggling fish that has stiffened. There's no doubt, she is what she pretends to be.

68

Go into the forest. It's very early, the forest is about to wake up, the soundless vibration of insect wings, song forming in the throats of birds, drops bursting with a membrane of slower time. A small, almost invisible tree cuts silence in two. When the light lifts its baton only half the forest joins in, the rest always belongs to darkness.

69

In late winter the light advances, fog is torn apart in the forest, but it is still grey. Even when the wind is calm the trees start to dance, shaking their short skirts so the snow slips off. Suddenly they stand green and naked in the cold. The sight of them makes the heart hammer, slowly. The heart is a bear's den in a forest far away.

70

They are not hiding on the steps in order to drink the early sunlight nor have they forgotten themselves. They thrust out their chins and swallow as much as they can. Some of the light spills out, but they quickly wipe themselves dry with rough, hard fingers. She places her hand on a warm patch on her hair, the businessman sucks up sun until his lips burn. The third one sits with his back to the sun, not for long, just until he feels a direct stab.

71

Petrification has set in, but the picture doesn't seem to weigh anything. The pale linen cloth floats above the table-top, the jug with flowers of snow balances on a patch of sunlight. A salt shaker, a glass of water, all the petrified things, a newspaper, a doll with a white torso, touch each other with their mouths.

72

There was so much that he wanted. But, exposed to the world, he was left standing on a pavement in the city a long time ago, helpless, shoulder to shoulder with the huge instrument in an unwieldy case. How can he carry it by himself, while holding an umbrella and crossing the road? It's a riddle. He is captured in the rain.

73

Snow has fallen, even though it's spring. The street lamps are extinguished. One morning they wake up to war, and now the lights will stay dark for many years. The cars have stopped, only a cycle-taxi fights its way through the chaos. Perhaps the news has not yet reached the few pedestrians who have ventured out. Yet they are on their toes. It suddenly makes sense that they are so vigilant.

74

She bends down, but the top of her head is still blocked by the picture frame. A chandelier swings behind her. Her hair, her raised shoulders, the table she leans against, are all slanting and about to crash. Everything spins slowly round an invisible centre. Her angry face and naked torso almost touch the lens when they fly past. When the door is off its hinges and a wall cracks children bawl silently.

75

She points the lens into the darkness, tries to focus on a tree she is convinced is right in front of her, on a headland. It's somewhere near here. Then she waits and finally falls asleep, but still keeps standing with her finger on the shutter until the morning mist rises from the tarn. Some time during the night it happens, she takes a picture of the dream tree just as the clouds are ripped away from the moon.

76

Over there war rages, but here on the other side of the silvery sea, no great distance, she photographs the sunset, which makes it look as if the white sun loungers are flying over the black sand. They don't cast shadows, they receive the muted applause of the waves. Even though the image is showy, it will endure.

77

The tree in Prague is far away and not far at all. It stands in front of a window in a timeless enclave, a peaceful garden, where the eyes can rest. The sun has wrapped it in white light, sealed it with silver and retouched the shadow, replaced with a black crevice in the ground. A fruit tree with buds, stopped before they could unfold, not shrivelled, not dead, but transformed into an image of longing.

78

The rain is heavy but lifts just long enough to reveal the overloaded car in front of the gas station. Miraculously the windows also clear for a moment so that the children's faces, dead tired and bewildered, make an impression. Take a closer look. This is not a vacation, but a vehicle for flight. How many people are there? You catch a glimpse of a teddy bear, pans, a spade, a rifle too, before the windows steam up.

79

With his back to the light which streams from the depths or pierces the surface, he floats upside down in order to be reunited with his shadow. It's hard to know what is up or down in the picture without instructions or a frame. The shadow curls its feet and stretches its hands out to him, or the other way round. They are ideas that flicker on the border of sleep, but they are not ideas.

80

The overlapping folds are neither a dress nor a curvaceous nude with a cool surface. The figure does not bend its head in prayer or shame. The picture does not depict a mother standing with her back turned, neither in a literal nor an abstract sense.

81

The apple in this picture is far from perfect. It's deeply pitted and scabbed, while the flesh is pulpy and cold, even though the fruit is lying in yellow, lukewarm grass, absorbing the last of the autumn sun. It's holding tight to the juice which trickles out through holes bitten by insects or mice, but it's only a few small, sticky drops. You can still feel that burst of acidic satisfaction in the head, and sweet fatigue spreading through your jaw—if you close your eyes.

82

These are her photos of Lake Koshkonong, on a day when the sun lights up among trees rooted in grey ice. The ice is fragile at the edges, like the crust on a wound. Behind the trees you can just make out the cabin with all that she owns, threatened by flood waters every spring. Like the ice, the photo keeps everything in place for a while. And the picture exposes the silence, but if you listen long enough it will break into a roar.

83

I will produce more snow, which got lodged in the cracks between the flagstones, stop the powdery layer on the lawn from melting, return blue light to the black bushes and a yellow tinge to the white when darkness falls and the afternoon is here. I will invoke the smell of something that doesn't smell of anything because it's too cold, and a chill that grips the hands and a smooth, stiff forehead. I will show you a white cloud of breath against the sky before it's too late. Could a photograph do better?

84

The photograph travels. It can be found in several places at once, but with its warm smile and glossy hair it is out in the world as my representative, without deception or design. It shows me the way I was. It's not that long ago.

85

The sun is low in the picture, yet it lifts windows off their hinges and removes ceilings and walls in a house that's about to give way to the disgrace of decay. The picture is very small, but in memory it's big enough to be true to life, in memory it represents a home, even though snow is falling in broken mirrors and, on the floor, black mould blooms.

86

Then one late summer evening the stillness of the image coincides with the subject. After we have called in the children and the dogs, closed the garage and all the doors, everything goes quiet. The whirr of moths and snap of twigs are faint sounds, or perhaps an illusion.

List of Images

41: Margarethe Mather: 'Untitled (Open Door), 1928'.
42: Henri Cartier-Bresson: 'Rue Mouffetard, Paris, 1954' and 'Paris vu de Notre Dame, 1955'.
43: Henri Cartier-Bresson: 'Juvisy, 1955', 'Foire du Trône, Paris, 1952', 'Leningrad, 9 Mai 1972', 'Texas, 1961' and 'Joinville-le-Pont, 1938'.
44: Henri Cartier-Bresson: 'Hyères, 1932' and 'Kite festival, Ahmedabad, India, 1966'.
45: Henri Cartier-Bresson: 'L'Isle-sur-la-Sorgue, 1988'.
46: Vippetangen 1942. *Aftenposten* archives. Quote from Gunvor Hofmo, 'Your Heart' (*Posthumous Poems*, edited by Jan Erik Vold).
47: Robert Doisneau: 'Paris 1944', 'Amour et barbelés au jardin des Tuileries', Paris, 1944.
48: Henri Cartier-Bresson: 'Auto-portrait, Italia, 1932'.
49: Robert Doisneau: 'La Voiture fondue, 1944'.
50: Ahlam Shibli: from Palestine, probably 2006.
51: Dora Maar: 'Garçon avec un chat dans les bras, appuyé contre une vitrine, 1935' and 'Enfant faisant le poirier sur le sable'.
55: Francesca Woodman: 'Untitled, Summer 1972'.
57: Henri Cartier-Bresson: 'Sevilla, 1933'.
58: Bill Brandt: 'Housewife, Bethnal Green, 1937'.
59: Henri Cartier-Bresson: 'Nude, Italy, (Leonor Fini),1933'
60: Virginia Woolf: from 'Blue & Green', *Monday or Tuesday, Eight Stories* Kessinger Publishing's Rare Reprints, 2010.
61: Francesca Woodman: 'Untitled, Providence, Rhode Island, 1978'.
62: Francesca Woodman: 'Providence, Rhode Island, 1976'.
63: Jane Evelyn Atwood: from *Too Much Time, Women in Prison*, 2000.
64: Andrei Tarkovsky: 'Tonino is an angel', 'Just outside Bagno Vignoni, Italy, 1979-82.
65: Jitka Hanzlova: from the series 'Forest', 2002.
66: Francesca Woodman: 'Then at one point I did not need to translate the notes: they went directly into my hands, Providence, Rhode Island, 1976' and 'Untitled, Providence, Rhode Island, 1975-1978'.
67: Francesca Woodman: 'From Angel Series, Rome, 1977'.
68: Jitka Hanzlova: from the series 'Forest', 2002.
69: Jitka Hanzlova: from the series 'Forest', 2002.
70: Henri Cartier-Bresson: 'Istanbul, 1965'.
71: Andrei Tarkovsky: 'San Gregorio, 24th November 1983'.
72: Robert Doisneau: 'Un musicien sous la pluie, Maurice Baquet, Paris 1957'.
73: Robert Doisneau: 'Vélo-Taxi, Avenue de l'Opéra, Paris 1942'.

74: Letizia Battaglia: 'Siciliana', 1970s.
75: Jitka Hanzlova: from the series 'Forest', 2002
76: Martine Franck: 'Club Méditerrané, Agadir, Marokko, 1976'.
77: Josef Sudek: 'The Window of My Studio, 1940-54'.
78: Dorothea Lange: California 1940. Drought refugees from Oklahoma.
79: Frank Eydner: 'Brückenspringer, 2007'.
80: Edward Weston: 'Pepper No 4, 1930'.
82: Lorine Niedecker: photo from Black Hawk Island, early 1960s.
83: Still from the film *Sylvia*, Christine Jeffs, 2004.
85: Francesca Woodman: 'Self-deceit #7, Rome, 1976' and 'Untitled, New York, 1979'.
86: Robert Adams: from 'Colorado Springs, Colorado, 1968'.

Select Bibliography

Giovanni Chiaramonte, Andrei A. Tarkovsky, *Instant Light, Tarkovsky Polaroids,* Thames & Hudson, 2006
John Berger, *Hold Everything Dear*, Pantheon Books, 2007
Jean-Claude Gautrand, *Robert Doisneau*, Taschen, 2003
Ian Jeffrey, *Bill Brandt*, Thames & Hudson, 2007
Jean-Pierre Montier, *Henri Cartier-Bresson, Seine Kunst – Sein Leben*, Schirmer/Mosel, 2002
Josef Sudek, *The Window of My Studio*, Torst, 2007
Chris Townsend, *Francesca Woodman*, Phaidon, 2008

Translator's Note

My translation is based on one by Hanne Bramness, as well as the original Norwegian text. I have also looked at the relevant photographic images when they exist in the public domain, and this has influenced my version of some of the prose poems.

Frances Presley
February 2013

The Author

Hanne Bramness is a poet, editor, translator and novelist. Born in 1959, she published her first collection of poetry, *Korrespondanse,* in 1983, followed by eight other collections. Three of them—*Kysset* (The Kiss,1998), *Trollmåne* (Troll Moon, 2001) and *Solfinger* (Sun's Finger, with illustrations by Laurie Clark, 2012)—are for children and young people. In 2007 Shearsman Books published a selection of her poems in English, *Salt on the eye, selected poems* (translated by Frances Presley and the author) and in 2008 her selected poems appeared in Norwegian, *Det står ulver i din drøm* (Wolves are standing in your dream). In 2003 she published the novel *Lynettes reise* (Lynette's journey; partly based on the early life of Welsh-Argentinian poet Lynette Roberts.) *Uten film i kameraet* (No film in the camera) was published in 2010.

Her numerous translations include works by William Blake, Mina Loy, Kamala Das, Denise Levertov, Selima Hill and Frances Presley.

She won the the Norwegian Poetry Club Prize in 1996 and the prestigious Dobloug Prize from the Swedish Acadamy in 2006. In 2012 she was awarded Wergeland's Oar, a prize for her work in poetry.

She lives by the Hardanger Fjord and in Berlin, and runs the small publishing company Nordsjøforlaget (The North Sea Press: www. nordsjoforlaget.no).

The Translator

Frances Presley is a poet, with several volumes to her name. The majority of her work up until 2009 was gathered in three volumes: *Paravane* (Salt Publishing, 2004), *Myne – new and selected poems & prose 1975-2006* (Shearsman, 2006), and *Lines of sight* (Shearsman, 2009). Since then two collaborative collections have appeared: *Stone settings* (with Tilla Brading), and *An Alphabet for Alina* (with Peterjon Skelt). A further volume, *Halse*, will appear from Shearsman in 2014. She lives in London.

www.ingramcontent.com/pod-product-compliance
Lightning Source LLC
Chambersburg PA
CBHW022200080426
42734CB00006B/519